Magnetic North

poems by

Lee Passarella

Finishing Line Press
Georgetown, Kentucky

Magnetic North

ACKNOWLEDGMENTS

The poems in this volume first appeared in the following publications, sometimes in different versions:

Antietam Review: "Racing the Storm"; *Blueline*: "Dahlias"; *Chattahoochee Review*: "Equinox"; Chelsea: "New Oak Leaves"; *Cream City Review*: "Nachtstücke"; *Electric Acorn*: "Autumn Song: Pathetic Verity"; *Elk River Review*: "Spring Song in South Georgia"; *Gaia*: "Winter as Sibyl"; *Kentucky Review*: "In a Rothko Landscape"; *Mankato Review*: "Thoughts, Mostly of You, from Charleston at Christmas"; *Penn Review*: "Starry Day"; *Piedmont Literary Review*: "Song: Night Wings"; *The Small Pond Magazine of Literature*: "Restoring the Fairmount Water¬works"; *Snake Nation Review*: "Judas Trees"; *Tar River Poetry*: "Trompe l'oeil"; *Whole Notes*: "Relativity"; *The Windless Orchard*: "Magnetic North."

Editor: Christen Kincaid

Cover Art: Lee Passarella

Author Photo: Katie Lynn Cochran

Cover Design: Elizabeth Maines

Printed in the USA on acid-free paper.
Order online: www.finishinglinepress.com
also available on amazon.com

Author inquiries and mail orders:
Finishing Line Press
P. O. Box 1626
Georgetown, Kentucky 40324
U. S. A.

Table of Contents

For Candace

Trompe l'oeil

i
Around the edges of the lawn,
raw and saw-toothed
as swamp grass—arrowhead
and cattails—a few live blades meander,
green verge to the lawn's sere river.
It's a logjam of pale, spent tubes,
the ghostly DNA that tells us
grass is bamboo's minute and distant cousin.

ii
This February morning,
the river's frozen over.
The treetops' high clerestory
sifts the new light into beams like lasers.
They unthread the dazed web
of frost that night has left behind
to snare the eye.

They burnish each cold spicule
until the yard's awash
in pearls, pearlescence—
for just a twinkling,
before a good jolt of perspective
frees the eye of its mistake.

Equinox

Wind shakes the colors
loose, patterns uncomplicated
from the folds of the quilt
that is spread: the soft architecture
of new poplar leaves, scalloped
and gothic; the dogwoods'
pilled flowers, knotted
wool; the labial wings
on the maples fingered coral,
red. But the pin oaks grab
their browns around them,
unwashed, *Lent* a word
small and blunt as any ritual.

You preach the creed
a thousand thousand times,
and always the same,
only rearranging the dust,
covering dead follicles
with a lie of green:
henna and celadon.
Somewhere the snow
remains—brittle, a wafer;
the grass drinks from it,
learning the hard lessons.

Spring Song in South Georgia

The gestural intensity of a day
like this seems rehearsed:
the mare's tails are clouds
out of genre painting, studied,
perfected, mass produced at last.
The star magnolias too numinous/
numerous, the daffodils too Crayola-
yellow, even naturalized.

Spring needs to be spontaneous,
as in West Philly, South Boston,
or the Bronx: the nude ailanthus
contemplating heaven from the alley
way, the gutter ice floes lovingly
sculpted in the black basalt
of cinders and exhaust. Then,
like the survivor of some private
Holocaust, the lone striped crocus
in the park the city forgot it owns.

Europa and the Bull

For some, just another weekday: Workmen
rebuild the pavilion at the park, stapling
tar paper, snapping chalk lines, hammering
as earnestly as the ochre letters on the sign
board beside the river:
              NO WADING OR SWIMMING
                    THESE WATERS
                    ARE DANGEROUS
Indifferent, the black Lab prows the deepest
parts—calm as tea, bijou/Gulf-Coast green—
retrieving his tossed branch. Here and there,
fly casters fight the current to stay upright,
walk half a dozen rocks, wade out where
they can see their prey, eye, patience,
and at last a little muscle, little as possible,
engaged. As with the young sunbathers
on their rock out in the middle, she
in her bright, scant suit—knees raised,
spread to take the sun as she will, him tonight.
Beside her, maybe he dreams of it
as he sponges sun, bare back dazzled,
as much of white as you can see
in this place of blotter-paper tans
and greens. Except the infrequent
culet the rocks cut as the river glances
at them, through channels like the sun visors
on old cars, that kind of green, that kind
of clear, the current hard enough to slice
through anything it finds: mud, grit,

rock, eventually, to show the business
that it means. But for the moment,
in that part of the mind that sees
exactly what it wants, yang turns to yin,
earth gets the upper hand, the outcrops
like some river-plying giant heading north,
away from the sea and surcease, trailing
wakes in a hundred different places.
The few lucky ones ride
the backbone of the beast,
gravity just another law to be ignored.

Judas Trees

Not sanguinary
but royal Tyrian—
each branch a black
rain sop bulged
and broken like a twist
of old telephone
wire with the insulation
worn through
until the words show,
mauve, electric,
shouting
from the oaks'
dank umbra:

the aptness of mad
Pound's petal faces
in the crowd
now understood.

Magnetic North

University of South Florida, St. Petersburg

It was a tiny inlet cut out
of the land, concreted, pinned down
at its corners by boxy structures
like the landmarks on a map
you'd sketch to give someone directions.
I was eating lunch there, soaking up
the sun, when I overheard two students
having their professors for lunch:
It could only be two pages
the one girl said *and it needed all these*
references! Like, how can you get Socrates
and Plato and the Skeptics and the Sophists
in two pages? I mean, my intro could have been
two pages!
        I silently agreed,
and also agreed it could be done
in one good paragraph
and that her despair masking
vanity would make one funny,
little poem. Then her friend said
A dolphin! and again ten seconds later
I'm telling you, I'm not seeing things!
Then fifteen more and we were all believers,
the blue steel of his dorsal fin carving
a space so small there wasn't even room
for its wake.
        Just 50 feet from us—
in that improbably small place
between Library and boat slips, between snack bar

and Museum—the bemused features
like an embryo's, the dark tundra he dredged
up as he spilled back into that cold
magnetic pole he inhabited,
the places where words aren't wanted.

Relativity

The woods have raised
a tabernacle so intact,
the light appears to come
in only at a flap.

It lies in widely
constellated coins
the perfect shape
of last year's leaves

or the rumpled knuckle of a limb.
I know it's just a trick,
like the red/gold fire
of a lake you see

in passing from a plane.
In lame reality,
the sun moves west
as always, I stay

as always in my place,
under the unabiding tent
in shade; nothing is changed
by the coining of the light.

In a Rothko Landscape

Late October, Donegal Springs, Pennsylvania

Cows low, invisible in a fog as thick
as soup base: milk and water. Their voices
are immediate, cupped in the dense-wet

air, offered as a fact you can't avoid,
their smell ripe as an ancient barnyard
in this airless bell of vapor. Even the leaves

are milked of their savor, fall as sound only,
amplified. Near the eponymous springs,
a dump of broken mailboxes, packing cases,

the dark bones of departed farm tools.
And in the angle of the fence, a yellow
chaise, almost new—a front-row seat

to nothing. It is a canvas of white and
black, with one screaming-yellow smudge,
lacking the complacency of any sorrow.

Autumn Song: Pathetic Verity

It's the season of gold and blood,
whose intricate frescos might almost
tell a human tale, the old one
about the flesh and spirit. The beech tree
sifts its coins through knotted fists;
the dogwood turns to a fountain
of blood, becomes shorthand
for Medea, Tarquin, the Son of Sam.
Or the obverse of that well-worn coin:
tree of the Crucifixion made
Lamb of God. In the golden afternoons,
our tongues roll round
appropriately Latinate syllables:
impasto, imprimatura….

Might *almost* tell the tale,
but doesn't. Neither Van Eyck
nor Pollock, abstract *and* inexpressive,
it's the season of colored sugar water,
the placebo we drink with our eyes
against the coming blankness,
that long dry spell in the marrow.

Starry Day

I'm sitting in one of the dark
mansions of the heart.
It's cold and dry here,
like the field where a child
might go to try out the toys
he gets on Christmas day. I can
imagine that field from where I sit,
as you can piece together a world
from the jeweled rags of light
and shadow a bright day will throw
against the wall when you're sick in bed

—straw nodding above the junk
and rutted mud. White on gray,
on gray, to the bruise-
blue of the farthest edge,
where field becomes a moat,
or mood, around the shuttered
factories of Yeadon and West Philly.

The metallic patchwork
of the windows, gratings, vents
shimmers with bezeled wealth,
a something to be prized—
a Starry *Day*, a Mondrian retelling
of van Gogh, even to the arthritic
jointedness of the many-
scarred ailanthus trees. They
dog the corners of my vision
like a living frame to what I see.

Wind kites the whited
newsprint on its invisible strings.
I launch my jet or rocket,
whatever it is I got that day.
And it becomes part
of an oddly beautiful cosmology,
the quaint design
I lived by then.

Winter as Sibyl

A month ago terrapins and sliders clumped
like galls on half-sunk limbs. They've had
enough of summer now, taking the sun
only when coming up for air, nosing the surface
like breathless fish in a slow ground
to the dragonflies' scat-sung counterpoint.

Accept the lake for what it is now:
an inland ocean choked with shoals of algae.
They smear and trail in spongy clots,
tear limb from limb the mirrored trees
that in another season could fall whole, weightless
as shades into an underworld of tarnished light.

Stuck in the green continuum that's August,
it's hard to think winter might come again,
sponge fishing, unraveling each billowed thread.
Working its slow work at the bottom:

riffling the stacks and reams of leavings,
writing chapters, whole novels,
on the latticed skeletons.

Thoughts, Mostly of You, from Charleston at Christmas

The new river park is about as quaint
as you'd expect—arcades with swings,
promenades, fountains, one in the form of a pineapple
exploded, a wry symbol of hospitality, its scored
brass husk and leafy topknot looking anxious
to part company on sun-bronzed jets. But at low tide,
the Cooper River seemed even shallower than it was,
drained of history like its smeared banks:
here, an aircraft carrier in mothballs
for the tourist trade; there, an idle crane or two,
a craning bridge straddling the bay on fowl's legs—
that was all. Except that some TV station paid
homage to the season, a tiny triangle of lights
(*o tannenbaum!*) lost high on an antenna
over Patriot's Point. Uptown,
the steeples very real against a latticed sky,
pink and blue barred like old townhouse windows
with their hurricane gear in place. One pink
streamer reached from white Saint Michael's
north to Saint Phillip's sandy spire, honed
to a gilt-edge sheen by spotlights hidden
around cornices and eves. Now a pennant,
salmon-orange, and just as quickly a banner,
blood-red, before the light failed at the peaked lid
of the horizon. At the Huguenot Church
the chorus had struggled with "For Unto Us"
above their wheezy organ, while overhead
this one red ribbon lapped the whole sky,
bloodying the river, the fountains,

suggesting, what, to those who swung
on swings or walked the riverwalk?
a foretaste of Resurrection? the lamb
with its bloody pennon of victory
as in those Old Masters, always
so full of blood—buckets, cisterns,
spillways of the all-sufficient stuff?
Probably not; just a pleasant evening,
a good time for trysts after last-minute shopping.

No victory. Not even stalemate.
Just a lonely thought inside one head,
when I would rather share your thoughts
under that sheeted Northern sky.

Restoring the Fairmount Waterworks
Philadelphia, July 1990

After the Art Museum, haunted
by its unquiet ghosts of modernism—
Dali, Miró, Tanguy all in black moods
echoing behind my eyes—I walked
the ramp down from Faire Mount
past a row of smashed and sunken
streetlamps, garlanded, beMused,
trash now, anachronisms when they were made
ages ago (in the dog years
that mark the life of American cities),
down a broken well of stairs ingrown
with weeds, beer-can littered, the stack-
blackened rocks primed white here
and there with jazzy graffiti. Below,

the restorers were putting the finishing
touches on the Waterworks:
Greek temple colonnades just for show
and proper sight lines, flanked by two
outbuildings that must have housed
the works, airy yet substantial, something
of the virgin *and* the dynamo happily
coexisting in these Greek rival
sheds of green and pink pastel.
On one side old William Rush's river
goddess, pristine in white painted
wood, blesses the wide gray sewer
she's come to represent. Across

the Schuylkill, where the boys
from Mantua still fish with the reek
of a million upstream flushes in their nostrils,
the Expressway and West River Drive
roar along tiered like mock gardens
in a blue tailpipe haze. Yet here,
beneath the place art goes
to die, the restorers work in loving
impervious strokes, building on a human
scale again, hinting at the tricks
the light plays in a sylvan place
—quick, lepidoterous—
in splashes of white, green,
and pink pastel, countless ages
from the Schuylkill that old Rush
knew, miles and endless ages
from Seurat's Grande Jatte.

Racing the Storm

*In this enchanted mood, thy spirit ebbs away to
whence it came....—Moby-Dick, "The Mast-Head"
—for Jack*

The story was an Ishmael's tale
I'd told a dozen times:
how we took off into that storm
we hadn't seen, and how
you got us through it.
As if the string of terrors
and the fear of dying
was all there was to it.
But there was more I didn't
or couldn't tell: what I'd learned
about risks and those who take them.
The *why*—about the adrenaline,
and the dark place where a form
of confidence is born....

We hung on updrafts,
wind shear tugging at the stick
with the fight of a game fish.
The west was a black cave's mouth
where the Flint River slid away
on bronzed scales, then disappeared.
But out in front of us,
the east lay open, glazed lakes
placed like stepping stones
to the edge of seeing.
I remember how you wondered
if we should land the little plane
or try to outrun the storm
that dragged us back
with the cold twinge
of momentary weightlessness

you feel in the pit
of the pit of your stomach.

And then the river parted
to share its mysteries with us,
as if the rotor of some giant
hovercraft had scooped it out:
whitecaps, long combers
riding to the banks, then back again
to the center. Right there,
beneath the chop
and froth, the calm dark space
we'd never guessed at,
alluring as a boy's dream
of those hallowed
nether parts of woman.

Come home, it said to me,
but you'd have none of that,
of desperately telling the bright beads,
deciphering the golden runes
the earth spread out ahead of us,
until we'd beat the storm,
or it beat us. Of letting whatever happens,
happen. But in that cavernous second
when we hung suspended
between the up- and downdrafts,
and the black water said, *Come home*,

you chose for us instead
the course of dull unfaith.

Of Beethoven's Harp Quartet

The pizzicato figure in the first thematic group
gives Opus 74 its nickname, "The Harp,"

though

Mandolin or *Guitar*, even *Harpsichord*,
any plucked not struck or dragged-on instrument
would do for a name if that's all that mattered.
Any publisher can coin a phrase that sells, name
a thing if a name is all you want.

But *Opus 74*

will always be more than a thing above a name
plaque in a museum, a marble paradigm:
the wild explosion of that sweet first theme
in the development—syncopated phrases
jagged as shrapnel, a crazy canon double forte
over tremolos: the classic mold is broken,
marble's taught to do new tricks, comes to life
as in the old, dead myth. But here the myth's
rewritten; the sculpture finally gives in,
takes the sculptor to her as she would the blade,
dangerous and exacting, takes him as any once-
cautious lover would who quits a safe but
deadly marriage, who learns the best marriages
aren't made in heaven after all.

Memento Mori

i
For the Elizabethans, the act of love
was a death in little.
How they must have cherished death,
to consider that most intimate,
and animate, of acts a practice run for dying.
Death would need to be something realer,
and much more lovely, for us to love it now
as much as that.

ii
From our window, we can see the wreckage
of two barely living maples
at the corner of the motel parking lot.
Long finger bones point at us
through the armature of green. Below,
the cowed trunks are wound with ancient ivy,
as if to hold the dying wood together.

Standing entwined by the window,
our bodies aren't perhaps as young
as they once were, but just as willing—
the bed a sweaty tangle from the lovemaking,

and death, for us, a token unreal
as those dead fingers
lost against the backlit sky.

Dahlias

A light wind takes the old woman's
handiwork in hand: Sunburst,
Star of Bethlehem, Grandmother's
Flower Garden—the quilts loll
on their clothesline, a rural
art display. My wife cursorily
takes in the big picture
each canvas unfolds—the play
of garish color within the straitened
four walls of an irrefragable
geometry. Then, like a connoisseur
getting down to where a painting
lives, she analyzes brushstrokes:
turns each quilt, numbers
for me the stitches per inch,
explains how, like a race driver
taking a curve more smoothly
than his peers, the winning quilter
stitches as evenly on the curves
as on the straightaway.

Later, we catch a glimpse
of the garden peering at us
from behind the line with each tug
of wind. Fifty dahlias taller
than our heads, on stalks as thick
as sugar cane or green bamboo,
the flowers in colors lavish
as the quilts'—lavender, carmine,

puce, lemon, candy-stripe—
the petals big nests
of compass points, pleasing
in their rough geometry.
We praise them all they're worth.
The woman tells us they were
even prettier before last week's storm
tore them up. Self-evident,
a broken oak limb tall
as a young tree lies across
her yard, the outermost branches
fingering the closed-in porch.
"Looks like God watched over you,"
says my wife, the connoisseur.
And the woman quietly assents,
the old house rooted to its slender
verities: the white cat
marmoreal on his stoop,
the dahlias tossing up
their thousand ragged stars.

Nachtstücke

1.
Tonight, air and music
have the same atomic weight.
As in that lab experiment,
the ball filled with air
then airless,
you could place the air itself—
filled with, then bereft
of music—on a scale
and find it lost half its mass and heft.

2.
The way the music
pauses briefly on the sill,
silvered in the lamplight,
as if considering the moon
at the lip of a sluice,
before—dark with oil
as well-loved wood—
it falls and fingers
above the black glass of the lawn
to where you stand
ear-deep in night,
the light at the window
firing your hair.

Accommodation

Somebody loves us all.
—*Elizabeth Bishop, "The Filling Station"*

Somebody
has proffered to us
these thousand wild nosegays in shocking pink,
a meadowful of them. It's coffee-shop art,
all the more garish for its tastefully
rendered highlights in old gold,
its plain frame of slate-gray.
Severe: the colors of wet clouds
and autumn drought. The tall grass
nods pale heads, wise with seed.

Really, it's a ham-handed gesture,
like those wingèd putti
that sugarcoat the altarpieces
and frescos of Old Masters.
Fat, pink fish—they ply the air like waves
nuzzling the cloud
the Madonna sails through, always
with a slippery grin, an adoring stare. Eager,
nimble as gourami in a tank,
how they shadow the inscrutable,
the grim-faced saint
or the monumental and perfected Savior
swimming His way across
the white empyrean.

Song: Night Wings

My wife works the garden
after dark, white blouse,
bare arms defined by olive,
and by black. Hesitant moth

movement, white wings
of her shoulders folding
to her tool, showing the blade
where to fall between the rows.

Above, the feathery darkness
of her hair, like the moth's
soft-quilled antennae,
its extravagant second sight.

New Oak Leaves

haunt streetlamps,
their wings wet
with light, paralyzed
in the orbits they describe
as if wishing for the light
from an incapable beyond.
As if those windows
the lamps cut from the dark
were photographs
that held them forever
to the flame of their desire.

Then you walk through
those windows into darkness,
and the avenue wheels
with the beat
and the echoed
beat of wings.

Lee Passarella acts as senior literary editor for *Atlanta Review* magazine and served as editor-in-chief of Coreopsis Books, a poetry-book publisher. He also writes classical music reviews for *Audiophile Audition* and acts as associate editor for *Kentucky Review.*

Passarella's poetry has appeared in *Chelsea, Cream City Review, Louisville Review, The Formalist, Antietam Review, Journal of the American Medical Association, The Literary Review, Edge City Review, The Wallace Stevens Journal, Snake Nation Review, Umbrella, Slant, Cortland Review,* and many other periodicals and online journals.

Swallowed up in Victory, Passarella's long narrative poem based on the American Civil War, was published by White Mane Books in 2002. It has been praised by poet Andrew Hudgins as a work that is "compelling and engrossing as a novel." Passarella has published two poetry collections: *The Geometry of Loneliness* (David Robert Books, 2006) and *Redemption* (FutureCycle Press, 2014). His poetry chapbook *Sight-Reading Schumann* (Pudding House Publications) appeared in 2007. Passarella's first novel for young adults, *Storm in the Valley,* was published by Ravenswood Press in 2015. A sequel, *Cold Comfort, Ill Wind*—again, a historical novel based on the American Civil War—appeared in January 2016.

Lee Passarella received a B.A. and M.A in English literature from Temple University and a Ph.D. in English literature from the University of Pennsylvania.

www.ingramcontent.com/pod-product-compliance
Lightning Source LLC
LaVergne TN
LVHW091235080426
835509LV00009B/1289